DATE DUE

PRINTED IN U.S.A.

LIFE IN AMERICA

Comparing Immigrant Experiences

by Brynn Baker

Consultant:
Cindy R. Lobel, PhD
Associate Professor of History
Lehman College
Bronx, New York

CAPSTONE PRESS
a capstone imprint

Connect Books are published by Capstone Press,
1710 Roe Crest Drive, North Mankato, Minnesota 56003
www.capstonepub.com

Library of Congress Cataloging-in-Publication Data
Baker, Brynn.
Life in America : comparing immigrant experiences / by Brynn Baker.
pages cm. — (Connect. U.S. immigration in the 1900s)
Includes bibliographical references and index.
ISBN 978-1-4914-4128-2 (library binding)
ISBN 978-1-4914-4174-9 (pbk.)
ISBN 978-1-4914-4180-0 (ebook pdf)
ISBN 978-1-4914-7891-2 (reflowable epub)
    1. European Americans—History—20th century—Juvenile literature. 2.
European Americans—History—19th century—Juvenile literature. 3. Immigrants—
History—20th century—Juvenile literature. 4. Immigrants—History—19th century—
Juvenile literature. 5. United States—Emigration and immigration—History—20th
century—Juvenile literature. 6. United States—Emigration and immigration—
History—19th century—Juvenile literature. 7. Europe—Emigration and
immigration—History—20th century—Juvenile literature. 8. Europe—Emigration
and immigration—History—19th century—Juvenile literature. I. Title.
E184.E95B34 2016
304.8'40730904—dc23   201500453

Editorial Credits
Jen Besel and Mandy Robbins, editors; Sarah Bennett, series designer; Katy LaVigne,
layout artist; Wanda Winch, media researcher; Laura Manthe, production specialist

Photo Credits
Capstone: graphic elements; Corbis, 29, Bettmann, 8, 40, 42-43, Minnesota Historical
Society, 7, 35; Courtesy of The Bancroft Library, University of California Berkeley,
cover (top), 22; CriaImages.com: Jay Robert Nash Collection, 33; Granger, NYC, 5,
25, 27; Library of Congress: Prints and Photographs Division, 11, 12, 15, 17, 21, 37,
39; Nebraska State Historical Society, cover (bottom); Shutterstock: Valentin Agapov,
paper design; State Historical Society of North Dakota (00090-0012), 30-31; Wisconsin
Historical Society: Wisconsin Place Photographs, 1855-1970s, ID: 38665, 18

Printed in the United States of America in Stevens Point, Wisconsin.
042015   008824WZF15

TABLE OF CONTENTS

CHAPTER ONE

COMING TO AMERICA

The United States has always been a land of immigrants. Pilgrims came in the 1500s to start new lives. Businesspeople and religious leaders came in the 1600s to start new colonies. In the 1700s slave traders forced Africans to immigrate to the country to tend crops. The 1800s saw a boom of immigrants from Ireland and gold-seekers from China. But the number of immigrants who came to America's shores in the early 1900s was truly amazing. From about 1880 to 1920, nearly 30 million immigrants flooded into the United States.

Shipload after shipload of immigrants docked on America's East Coast. Most of the immigrants who arrived in the early 1900s came from southern and eastern European countries. They arrived from places such as Poland, Hungary, Italy, Germany, and Greece.

These new immigrants were young, often between 15 and 30 years old. Many spoke no English and had nothing but the clothes they brought with them and the change in their pockets.

The S.S. Konigin Luise was one of the many ships immigrants crowded onto to reach the United States in the early 1900s.

WHY PEOPLE CAME TO AMERICA

Several world events caused the major boom in immigration in the early 1900s. Many European countries were experiencing land shortages, poor economies, or war. People left their homelands to escape **discrimination** because of their race, religion, or political beliefs. Crops were failing and families were starving. People came to America in hopes of a better life.

Immigrants were attracted to the idea of independence in America. The Declaration of Independence says, "All men are created equal." It also promises, "Life, liberty, and the pursuit of happiness." People took comfort in these words. Newcomers believed America was a land of opportunity.

American recruiters helped spread the idea that opportunities were plentiful. Businesses sent recruiters to Europe, offering jobs to skilled workers. Railroad companies also advertised overseas. They promoted cheap farmland and work opportunities.

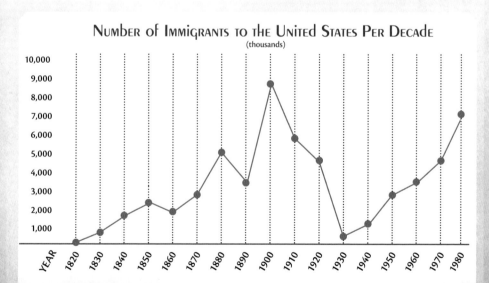

NUMBER OF IMMIGRANTS TO THE UNITED STATES PER DECADE
(thousands)

discrimination—treating people unfairly because of their race, country of birth, or gender

MINNESOTA!

CURE FOR THE PANIC

Emigrate to Minnesota!

Where no Banks exist; a supension is unknown. Land and Water of best kind. No Ague and Fever there. CLAIMS can be made by rich and poor.

THE MAN OF SMALL MEANS

CAN SOON REACH COMPETENCY.

Climate dry and healthy. The rich respect and assist the poor—all labor together. The finest Lands are open to pre-emption.

Saint Paul is the great stopping place,

From there you can go to any point, as emigrant settlers start daily to the various Land Offices and Districts.

T. B. W.

THOS. E. SUTTON, Printer, 142 Fulton Street, New York.

Advertisements such as this one boasting of the wonders of Minnesota drew immigrants to midwestern states.

Chapter Two

MISCONCEPTIONS OF AMERICA

Immigrants often called the United States "the promised land." They had heard false rumors of streets paved with gold. Many shared the belief that they would step off the ship to an easier life. They trusted that land, jobs, and higher wages waited for them.

Immigrants were also told stories of hope and beauty. "In America life is golden," sang Hungarian immigrant Renee Berkoff in 1922. "In America the flowers are more beautiful. In America the world is much better. And that is where I am longing to be my dear." However the reality of life in America was different than most expected.

City streets were crowded and chaotic. "The noise and all the languages were absolutely incomprehensible," recalled Stephen Peters, an immigrant who arrived in New York City in 1920.

Immigrants immediately faced challenges and discrimination. Many drifted into the slums of cities and worked for low wages. "I came to America because I heard the streets were paved with gold," said an Italian immigrant. "When I got here I learned three things. First, the streets are not paved with gold. Second, they weren't paved at all. And third, I was expected to pave them."

This New York City slum shows the type of living conditions many immigrants faced in the early 1900s.

TENEMENTS

With immigrants pouring in, cities became crowded, and many families were poor. Everyone needed a place to live. **Tenements** offered cheap rental apartments and housed many families. Most tenements were close to factories, docks, and slaughterhouses, which provided jobs for many immigrants.

The first tenement buildings stood side-by-side on narrow streets, with only a foot of space between them. They were dark and dusty because many did not have windows or proper air flow. Tenements did not have electricity or running water. Personal care was a major problem. People could not regularly bathe or wash clothing. Garbage and over-flow from outhouses covered the streets. "[Tenements] are great prison-like structures of brick, with narrow doors and windows, cramped passages and steep rickety stairs," described Jacob Riis, a journalist living in New York at the time.

This row of tenement buildings on Elizabeth Street in New York City shows the crowded living conditions of poor New Yorkers in the early 1900s.

tenement—a rundown apartment building

FIXING CONDITIONS

Journalist Jacob Riis photographed the horrible living conditions in the tenements on the Lower East Side of New York City. He published a book in 1890 called *How the Other Half Lives*. His book led to many changes. In 1901 New York City officials passed the Tenement House Law. Tenements were updated to include fire escapes, windows, and bathrooms. More than 200,000 new apartments were also built over the next 15 years to accommodate the growing population.

CITIZENSHIP

Immigrants who came to the United States in the early 1900s were not immediately legal citizens. They could live and work in America, but they could not vote. In order to become citizens, immigrants had to live in the United States for five years. Then they could file the paperwork for citizenship. After filing, they had to wait between one and three years before moving on to the next step. The second step was to go before a court and sign an Oath of Allegiance. Only after these steps were completed could immigrants be sworn in as legal citizens.

Many American citizens blamed the problems of the nation on the large immigrant population. This opinion was shown in political cartoons.

NATIVISM

Many immigrants arrived with next to nothing. They immediately needed housing and employment. Immigrants often took any job they could find, usually for low wages. Native-born Americans became frustrated because they had to compete with the immigrants for employment. Many employers cut costs by hiring immigrants, and citizens grew angry.

Native-born Americans in the 1900s spoke English and were mostly white, **Protestant**, and a part of America's growing democracy. Immigrants spoke many different languages. Most came from countries with failing governments and economies. The majority were also **Catholic**.

An idea called nativism began to take hold in the country. Nativism is the belief that people born in a country are better than immigrants. This idea affected the way people treated newcomers. It even affected the laws passed by Congress. Nativists believed "foreigners" would ruin America. They blamed immigrants for everything from lack of jobs to organized crime.

Protestant—a Christian who does not belong to the Roman Catholic or the Orthodox Church
Catholic—a member of the Roman Catholic Church

13

THE HATED IMMIGRANTS

The Irish were one of the first groups of immigrants to arrive. Many came before immigration numbers peaked in America. A potato famine in Ireland killed nearly 1 million people. Families were starving and out of work. They fled the country in huge numbers.

As many as 4.5 million Irish immigrants arrived in America between 1820 and 1930. Most Irish immigrants were Catholic, unskilled, poor, and unfamiliar with city life. Many citizens worried the Irish would destroy America's thriving democracy.

Irish immigrants were met with hatred. Citizens stood on the docks, throwing things at the Irish as they got off ships. Mobs and riots against these immigrants broke out in many cities in the northeast.

Irish immigrants also faced discrimination. "No Irish need apply," was common in job advertisements. Most Irish immigrants accepted jobs in the city that no one else wanted. They worked long hours for little pay, building bridges, roads, and canals. Some found jobs in the mining and quarrying industries.

◖◖ FACT ◗◗

New York was one of the many cities Irish immigrants flocked to. By 1860 one in four New Yorkers was Irish.

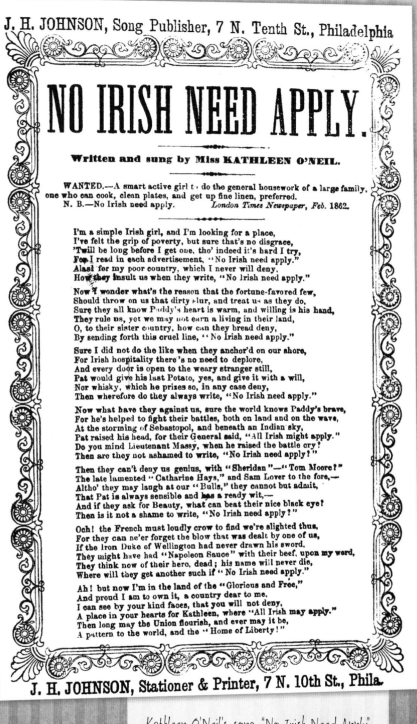

Kathleen O'Neil's song, "No Irish Need Apply" summed up the discrimination that many Irish immigrants faced in the early 1900s.

CHINESE IMMIGRANTS

People in China were dealing with overpopulation and poverty. When stories of the Gold Rush in California reached Asia in 1848, a large wave of Chinese immigrants arrived in the West. Most of these immigrants hoped to find their fortunes on "Gold Mountain," as they called California. They planned to return home as rich men.

But gold was hard to find. Many Chinese immigrants had to take other work. Labor recruiters for the Central Pacific Railroad hired 12,000 Chinese workers between 1865 and 1868. They were hired to lay track from California to Nebraska for the **Transcontinental** Railroad.

The country slipped into a depression after the completion of the project in 1869. Many native-born Americans blamed the Chinese immigrants for the economic downturn. When they returned to California, the Chinese became the targets of attacks and riots.

Nativism against the Chinese continued to grow. In 1882 Congress passed the Chinese Exclusion Act. This law stopped all Chinese immigration to America. It also prevented current Chinese immigrants from becoming U.S. citizens. After the Exclusion Act was passed, most Chinese immigrants had a hard time finding work. Many opened small businesses in Chinese neighborhoods known as Chinatowns.

transcontinental—going across a continent

When striking gold didn't work out, many Chinese immigrants found other ways to support themselves, such as this man selling goods in the street.

ᐸᐸ FACT ᐳᐳ

Chinese workers were not allowed to ride on the railroad they built. After it was completed, they were forced to walk back to California.

POLISH IMMIGRANTS

Polish immigrants were attracted to the higher wages and job opportunities available to unskilled laborers in America. A total of 2.5 million Polish immigrants arrived in the United States between 1860 and 1914.

Many of these immigrants had been farm laborers in Poland. However in America, they settled in midwestern cities. More jobs were available in industrial work than in agricultural. Polish immigrants worked in coal mines, steel mills, and slaughterhouses.

like many other ethnic groups, Polish immigrants found strength and comfort through settling into tightly-knit communities together.

DILLINGHAM COMMISSION

The U.S. government began to blame immigrants for ruining the economy. For example, by 1910 Polish immigrants had sent $40 million to relatives in Poland. In 1907 lawmakers formed the Dillingham Commission to study the effects of immigration in the United States. In 1911 the commission decided that immigration from southern and eastern European countries was a serious threat to America. The lawmakers recommended that immigration be reduced. The commission's findings provided the proof lawmakers needed to pass laws in the 1920s to restrict immigration.

Polish immigrants faced **stereotypes** that caused many shame. American-born citizens often joked that the Polish were known more for brut strength than for brains. "The Polacks are always strong," said Adam Labota, a Polish textile worker. "Many like to show how strong they are and they start throwing things and fighting."

Many Polish immigrants, especially their children, wanted to be accepted into American culture. "We were embarrassed if our parents couldn't speak English," explained Louise Nagy in 1913, daughter of Polish immigrants. "My father was reading a Polish newspaper, and somebody was supposed to come to the house. I remember sticking the newspaper under something. We were that ashamed of being foreign."

stereotype—an overly simple opinion of a person, group, or thing

RUSSIAN IMMIGRANTS

More than 3 million Russian **Jews** immigrated to America between 1881 and 1914. They came for freedom and hoped to find jobs. However many were met with the same hatred they had experienced at home. Native-born Americans did not like them for being different.

Five out of six Jewish immigrants settled in **urban** slums on the Lower East Side of New York. They quickly filled nearby clothing factories and shops. But there were more immigrants than jobs. They often ran sweatshops in their tenements. Women and children worked in dark and crowded rooms, making clothes by hand. Most worked 12 to 16 hours a day in extreme temperatures and unhealthy conditions. Jewish tenements became the heart of the city's clothing industry.

Jewish immigrants also worked selling goods from pushcarts on the streets of New York. They sold everything from collars and shoestrings to fresh meat and vegetables. Jewish salesmen were stereotyped as swindlers and cheats. "Many had to beg in order to survive," said George Price, a Russian immigrant.

Even immigrant children had to work to support their families, such as these girls who helped their mother make artificial leaves.

Jew—a person with a religion based on a belief in one God and the teachings of a holy book called the Torah

urban—having to do with a city

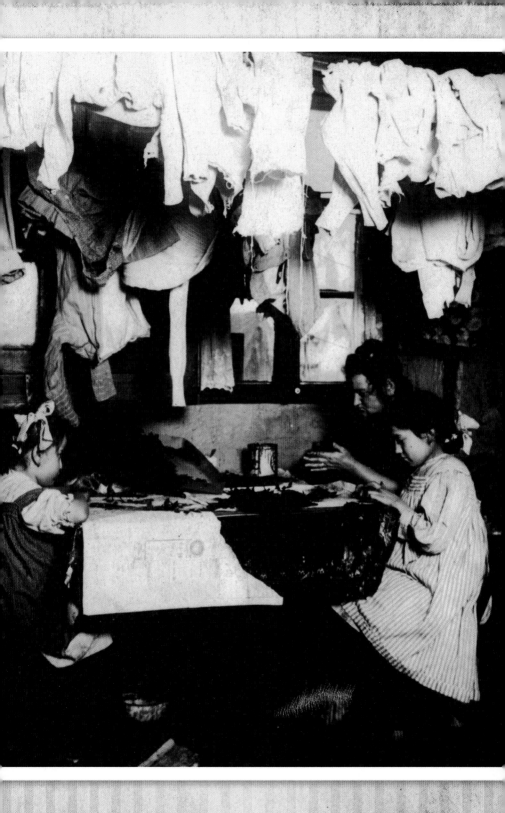

JAPANESE IMMIGRANTS

In the early 20th century, Japan's population was growing quickly. Cities were expanding, and the need for more factories took over. Many farmers lost their land. More than 100,000 Japanese immigrants arrived in America between 1900 and 1925. Many hoped to find peace and good fortune working the land.

Japanese farmers found abundant land to cultivate in America, especially in the state of California.

Japanese immigrants arrived on America's West Coast and settled in California. Many found work on the railroad, in lumber mills, mining camps, and canneries. However most worked as farmers.

Japanese farmers often rented land and small cabins out in the country. They worked hard, planting and tending farms, orchards, and vineyards. By 1920 Japanese immigrants controlled 450,000 acres (182,109 hectares) of California. Truck farming became a successful trade along the coast. Japanese farmers delivered fresh food to businesses, such as restaurants and hotels.

Despite their hard work, Japanese immigrants faced discrimination and racial attacks. American-born citizens and other immigrants envied the Japanese for their success. Angry mobs threatened the Japanese, driving many of them out of their homes.

CHAPTER THREE

BIRDS OF PASSAGE

Oftentimes immigrants came to America with the plan to someday return home. Historians call these people "birds of passage." Most of these temporary immigrants were men who left their families and friends in their homelands.

Austrian immigrants were among these "birds of passage." Factories were taking jobs and land away from Austrian farmers. Many of these farmers left, believing there would be land to farm in America. Most families stayed behind while the men went in search of work.

Two million Austrian immigrants arrived in America between 1900 and 1910. However most were disappointed. Many jobs in America had also become industrialized. These immigrants often ended up working in cities in the Northeast. They worked in steel mills, coal mines, stockyards, and cement factories. Most lived in tenements near their jobs.

Austrians were known to be very private, valuing comfort and family. Many tried to blend in to American culture to avoid unnecessary attention. They learned English and quickly adopted American traditions. But more than 35 percent of Austrian immigrants returned home to their families with their savings.

Austrian immigrants sacrificed their dreams of farming to work in steel mills, such as this one in Pittsburg, Pennsylvania.

GREEK IMMIGRANTS

Greece found itself in an economic standstill in the early 1900s. Many families sent their young sons to America to earn money. The boys were expected to return to Greece with money to buy land.

More than 400,000 Greek immigrants arrived in America between 1900 and 1920. Many worked in mines, mills, and meatpacking plants on the Northeast Coast and in the Midwest. Some also worked as dishwashers, shoe shiners, and street peddlers.

Most Greek immigrants planned to leave America eventually. But 70 percent of them ended up settling in the United States. Many had established successful businesses, including restaurants, grocery stores, flower shops, and hotels. Soon the men brought their wives and children to America. They brought with them the culture and social traditions of Greece. Communities grew rapidly around Greek Orthodox churches, schools, and coffee shops.

The Armour and Company meatpacking house in Chicago, Illinois, was one of the many places Greek immigrants found work.

ITALIAN IMMIGRANTS

Italian immigrants came to America by the thousands. In the early 1900s, Italy experienced many natural disasters that destroyed homes and farms. Poverty became widespread. People were not getting enough to eat and diseases were spreading.

More than 3 million Italian immigrants arrived in America between 1900 and 1915. They lived in cheap tenements in New York and Chicago. Most intended to work, save money, then return to Italy.

Italian immigrants experienced discrimination in the cities' workforce. Many employers thought Italians were too small and weak for construction. However, employers hired Italian immigrants because most would work for low wages. They became known as "strikebreakers" and "wage cutters." Italians dug canals and tunnels. They also laid railroad tracks and gas lines. Others built bridges, skyscrapers, and roads.

WORKING FOR A PADRONE

Many Italian immigrants came to America under the padrone system. A padrone was a person who recruited immigrants to come to America to work for employers. However, some padrones acted like slave owners. They told their immigrants where to work, controlled their wages, rationed their food, and watched everything they did. Some padrones even locked workers in guarded camps with barbed wire fences. Congress made the padrone system illegal in 1885. But the system continued illegally for many years after.

Many Italians became homeless after a devastating earthquake in 1908. They came to America by the boatload looking for a fresh start.

Chapter Four

SETTLING
THE MIDWEST

A large number of immigrants who came to the United States settled in the Midwest. There they built communities that allowed them to keep their languages and customs alive.

A total of 3.5 million German immigrants arrived in America between 1850 and 1880. They came looking to escape political unrest and a failing economy. Some settled in large cities such as New York, Milwaukee, Cincinnati, and St. Louis. However most chose to travel the Great Lakes and settle in the Midwest. Minnesota, Wisconsin, Iowa, North Dakota, South Dakota, and Nebraska became known as the "German Belt." Many German immigrants had agricultural backgrounds and came to work on farms. Home ownership was also highly valued. Many bought houses and land as soon as they could.

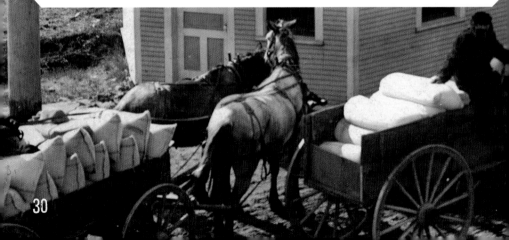

Family-operated businesses were also common. Children often dropped out of school to help their parents. Labor unions helped Germans achieve fair working conditions. They dominated the baking, brewing, and carpentry industries.

German immigrants faced discrimination from nativists too. Many of the immigrants had been political activists in their homeland. They had rebelled and started a series of revolts to establish a united Germany. But their actions had failed. The rebels feared they would be arrested or attacked, so they traveled to the United States. These German immigrants were highly educated. Nativists feared they would try to destroy American democracy.

◖ FACT ◗

German immigrants brought many Christmas traditions to America. The Christmas tree and gift-giving were traditions adopted into American culture.

SWEDISH IMMIGRANTS

In the late 1800s, people in Sweden were starving. Nearly 22 out of every 1,000 people died from famine. Crop failure caused many families to leave their homeland. Nearly 1.3 million immigrants made the journey from Sweden to America between the 1840s and 1920s.

Most Americans found the Swedish to be desirable immigrants. They were white, Protestant, and educated, like most native-born Americans. After their arrival, many city governments and companies recruited these immigrants to settle towns in the Midwest.

Swedish immigrants settled in Minnesota, Wisconsin, Illinois, Kansas, and Nebraska. But their daily life proved harder than they expected. Many recruiters had lied about the comforts and success of settler life. "None who are not accustomed to hard, agricultural labor ought to become farmers in this country," said a Swedish farmer living in Wisconsin. Many Swedish immigrants lived in log houses on large pieces of land. They had hard, labor-intensive workloads every day from sun up to sun down.

FACT

Minnesota became the state where most Swedish immigrants settled. In 1910 more than 12 percent of the state's population was Swedish-American.

An eager group of Swedish immigrants pose for a
photographer in Greeley, Kansas, in 1900.

NORWEGIAN IMMIGRANTS

In Norway the population was on the rise. Farmland became scarce. People were forced to leave in order to find work and food. When representatives from U.S. businesses went to Norway talking about jobs, many took the opportunity. More than 265,000 Norwegian immigrants arrived in the United States between 1880 and 1893.

Norwegian immigrants moved to the upper Midwest. They settled land in Minnesota, Wisconsin, Iowa, and the Dakotas. Many established towns and became successful farmers. Then they sent letters and money to their families in Norway. They wrote of their success in a country that treated them well. "A newcomer from Norway who arrives here will be surprised indeed," said Svein Nilsson, a Norwegian American journalist, "to find in the heart of the country, more than a thousand miles from his landing place, a town where language and way of life so unmistakably remind him of his native land." These letters encouraged more Norwegian immigration.

Norwegian immigrants such as Ole Graff and his son Halvor settled in Minnesota and became successful farmers.

Chapter Five

SMALLER GROUPS MAKE A BIG IMPACT

Immigrants came to the United States from all over the world. Some groups, such as the Germans and Norwegians, often stayed together. They took comfort in being with people from their own countries. Other groups spread far and wide, quickly adopting American customs.

In Scotland, much like in Norway, the population was booming. There wasn't enough farmland for everyone. Many Scottish immigrants came to America to find work. They settled in industrial cities all over New York, Illinois, Michigan, and Wisconsin.

Scottish immigrants fit in well with the majority of Americans, who were white and Protestant. Most earned a reputation for their confidence, hard work, and thrifty ways. They did not encounter much discrimination.

Scottish immigrants found work in large cities, such as this iron worker helping construct the Singer Tower in New York City.

CZECH IMMIGRANTS

Czech families left Europe to escape political and religious prejudices. They arrived in America between 1865 and 1914. They came for the freedom and land that life in America offered.

Czech immigrants settled all over the country. Many settled by the Great Lakes and on the Great Plains. Chicago had a large population of Czechs who worked as manual laborers. They cut down trees and hauled lumber, making space for new construction. Many Czech immigrants stayed in New York. They lived in tenements on the Lower East Side and worked as cigar makers. Some Czechs also traveled to the Midwest and established small communities of their own.

Czech immigrants were known to be free thinkers, valuing liberty and social equality. Many married into families of other ethnic groups. But preserving their culture, language, and traditions was still important to them. Many proudly wore folk costumes from their homeland.

Some Czech immigrants brought specialized skills with them, such as cigar-making. Everyone in the family, even children, pitched in for the family trade.

Czech—a person from the eastern European area of Czechoslovakia

Changing Names

To more easily fit into American culture, many Czech immigrants changed their last names when they arrived. Some last names were literally translated to English. For example, the name Krejčí became Taylor. The name Jablečník became Appleton. Others were changed to more American-sounding names. Vlk became the last name Wolf. Červený became Sweeney.

SWISS IMMIGRANTS

More than 90,000 Swiss immigrants arrived in America between 1890 and 1920. Many valued rural life and came to harvest land. They were looking for simple lives within peaceful communities.

Swiss immigrants settled in small towns in Wisconsin, Illinois, Ohio, Indiana, and Pennsylvania. Many chose to settle in the same areas as **Scandinavian** immigrants. Americans often confused Swiss immigrants for the French, German, or Italians. Many spoke more than one of the languages, in addition to their own.

Where Immigrants Came From

Russia
3,250,000

Austria / Hungary
3,700,000

England
2,500,000

Sweden
1,000,000

Norway - 730,000

Italy
4,190,000

Scotland - 570,000

France - 530,000

Greece - 350,000
Turkey - 320,000
Denmark - 300,000
Switzerland - 258,000
Portugal - 210,000
The Netherlands - 258,000
Belgium - 140,000
Spain- 130,000
Romania- 80,000
Wales- 75,000
Bulgaria- 60,000

Ireland
4,400,000

Germany
5,500,000

Swiss immigrants came from western Europe's oldest democracy. Many found American politics, culture, and lifestyles to be similar to Switzerland's. Most Swiss immigrants adapted to American life easily and were successful in many trades.

Like many families of the time, the Zahlers were large in number. Ida Zahler broughter her 11 children with her from Switzerland to America to join her father on his farm in Canton, Ohio.

Scandinavian—from the countries of Denmark, Norway, or Sweden

Chapter Six

NEW FACES, A CHANGED NATION

◖◖ FACT ◗◗

The new laws only allowed 350,000 European immigrants to enter the United States each year. Many Asian and African immigrants were not allowed to enter at all.

Immigrants came to America from all around the world. Their reasons for leaving their homes may have varied. But they all came for better lives. Most immigrants arrived with next to nothing. They needed to find homes and employment. Many encountered discrimination and had to overcome tough obstacles to succeed. But most did eventually thrive. Despite the hardships, very few gave up.

Immigration numbers began to drop at the beginning of World War I (1914–1918). In 1920 immigration slowed even further when the U.S. Congress passed laws limiting the number of people allowed into the country. But by then, the United States truly was a nation of immigrants. And those immigrants had changed the country forever.

TIMELINE

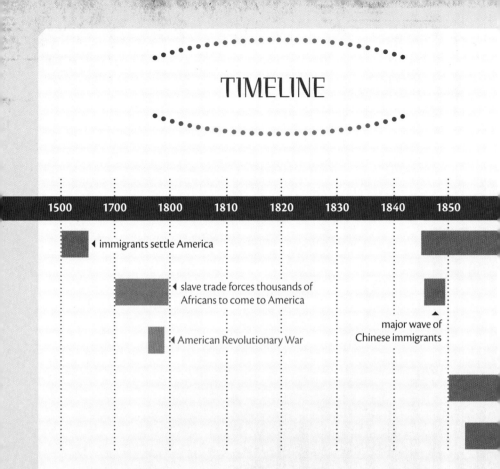

| 1500 | 1700 | 1800 | 1810 | 1820 | 1830 | 1840 | 1850 |

◄ immigrants settle America

◄ slave trade forces thousands of
Africans to come to America

◄ American Revolutionary War

▲
major wave of
Chinese immigrants

Had it not been for immigration during the early 1900s, America would be an entirely different country. Immigration had a direct impact on the country's growth and success. Immigrants were the muscle power needed to develop the nation. They were the farmers, miners, factory workers, and construction laborers who built the country. Immigrants were business owners, job creators, taxpayers, and consumers. They developed industries and grew the economy. Immigrants formed communities, built homes, and started families. They literally paved the road for future generations.

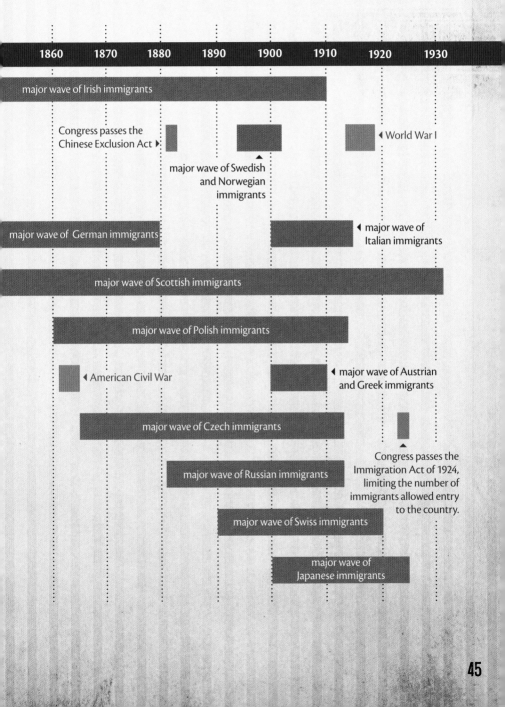

1860 1870 1880 1890 1900 1910 1920 1930

major wave of Irish immigrants

Congress passes the
Chinese Exclusion Act ▶ ◀ World War I

▲
major wave of Swedish
and Norwegian
immigrants

major wave of German immigrants ◀ major wave of
Italian immigrants

major wave of Scottish immigrants

major wave of Polish immigrants

◀ American Civil War ◀ major wave of Austrian
and Greek immigrants

major wave of Czech immigrants

▲
major wave of Russian immigrants Congress passes the
Immigration Act of 1924,
limiting the number of
immigrants allowed entry
to the country.

major wave of Swiss immigrants

major wave of
Japanese immigrants

GLOSSARY

Catholic (KATH-uh-lik)—a member of the Roman Catholic Church

Czech (CHEK)—a person from the eastern European area of Czechoslovakia

discrimination (dis-kri-muh-NAY-shuhn)—treating people unfairly because of their race, country of birth, or gender

Jew (JOO)—a person with a religion based on a belief in one God and the teachings of a holy book called the Torah

nativism (NAY-tuh-viz-uhm)—a movement that reflected preferences for native-born Americans and mistrust of immigrants

Protestant (PROT-uh-stuhnt)—a Christian who does not belong to the Roman Catholic or the Orthodox Church

Scandinavian (skan-duh-NAY-vee-uhn)—from the countries of Denmark, Norway, or Sweden

stereotype (STER-ee-oh-tipe)—an overly simple opinion of a person, group, or thing

tenement (TEN-uh-muhnt)—a rundown apartment building, especially one that is crowded and in a poor part of a city

transcontinental (transs-kon-tuh-NEN-tuhl)—extending or going across a continent

urban (UR-bun)—having to do with a city

READ MORE

Benoit, Peter. *Immigration*. Cornerstones of Freedom. New York: Children's Press, 2012.

Burgan, Michael. *Ellis Island: An Interactive History Adventure*. You Choose Books. Mankato, Minn.: Capstone Press, 2014.

Roza, Greg. *Immigration and Migration*. The Story of America. New York: Gareth Stevens Pub., 2011.

CRITICAL THINKING USING THE COMMON CORE

Compare the quotations from the Declaration of Independence on page 6 with the quotations from the immigrants on pages 9, 10, 19, 20, 32, and 34. How did the idea of America differ from the realities in America for most immigrants? *(Key Ideas and Details)*

Using other texts, explore how nativism influenced the laws that were passed in the United States in the 1900s. *(Integration of Knowledge and Ideas)*

INTERNET SITES

FactHound offers a safe, fun way to find Internet sites related to this book. All of the sites on FactHound have been researched by our staff.

Here's all you do:
Visit *www.facthound.com*
Type in this code: 9781491441282

INDEX